What's the Issue?

WHO ARE ENVIRONMENTAL ACTIVISTS?

By Jennifer Lombardo

KidHaven
PUBLISHING

Published in 2023 by
KidHaven Publishing, an Imprint of Greenhaven Publishing, LLC
2544 Clinton Street
Buffalo, NY 14224

Designer: Deanna Paternostro
Editor: Jennifer Lombardo

Photo credits: Cover (top) Hryshchyshen Serhii/Shutterstock.com; cover (bottom) oneinchpunch/ Shutterstock.com; p. 5 BlueRingMedia/Shutterstock.com; p. 7 Martyn Jandula/Shutterstock.com; p. 9 kotoffei/Shutterstock.com; p. 11 (background) Take Photo/Shutterstock.com; p. 11 (inset) Elime/ Shutterstock.com; p. 13 Sundry Photography/Shutterstock.com; p. 15 Roland Marconi/ Shutterstock.com; p. 17 Marti Bug Catcher/Shutterstock.com; p. 19 Diyana Dimitrova/ Shutterstock.com; p. 20 wavebreakmedia/Shutterstock.com; p. 21 alongzo/Shutterstock.com.

Cataloging-in-Publication Data

Names: Lombardo, Jennifer.
Title: Who are environmental activists? / Jennifer Lombardo.
Description: Buffalo, New York : KidHaven Publishing, 2023. | Series: What's the issue? | Includes glossary and index.
Identifiers: ISBN 9781534543706 (pbk.) | ISBN 9781534543720 (library bound) | ISBN 9781534543737 (ebook)
Subjects: LCSH: Environmentalism–Juvenile literature. | Green movement–Juvenile literature. | Environmentalists–Juvenile literature.
Classification: LCC GE195.5 L66 2023 | DDC 333.72–dc23

Printed in the United States of America

Some of the images in this book illustrate individuals who are models. The depictions do not imply actual situations or events.

CPSIA compliance information: Batch #CW23KH: For further information contact Greenhaven Publishing LLC at 1-844-317-7404.

Please visit our website, www.greenhavenpublishing.com. For a free color catalog of all our high-quality books, call toll free 1-844-317-7404 or fax 1-844-317-7405.

Find us on

CONTENTS

What's the Environment?

You probably hear a lot about the environment, but what exactly is it? It isn't just one thing. It includes everything in the natural world. Plants, animals, weather, dirt, ice, oceans—all of these things and more are part of the environment.

Everything in the environment is connected. If one thing changes, it creates changes in other parts of the environment. For example, if the soil in an area loses its **nutrients**, plants will have trouble growing there. The bees, birds, and other animals that use those plants for food will start to die, and so will the creatures that eat those animals.

Facing the Facts

Living things are often connected through food chains, which form as one living thing eats another. A food web is a series, or collection, of food chains in an environment. If one part of it changes, it will change all the other parts of the food web too.

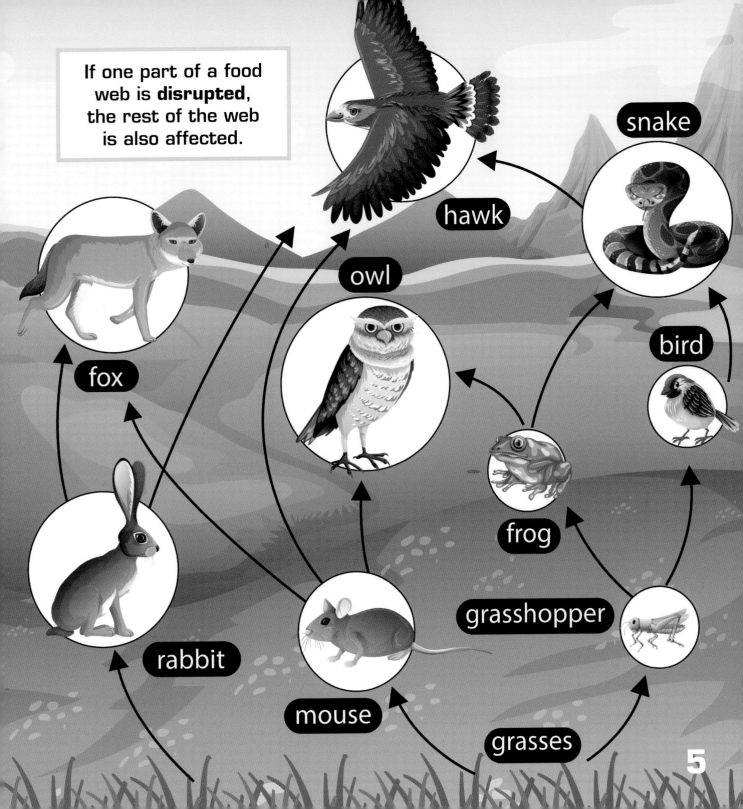

If one part of a food web is **disrupted**, the rest of the web is also affected.

snake

hawk

fox

owl

bird

frog

rabbit

grasshopper

mouse

grasses

5

The Environment in Trouble

Many hings change naturally in the environment. However, humans also cause a lot of changes that aren't natural. Many forms of **transportation** and factories pollute the air and water. People cut down huge areas of forest so cows have more grass to eat. With fewer trees to hold the soil together, it often dries up and blows away.

Environmental activists are people who are working to fix these and other problems. One of the ways they do this is by asking governments to pass laws that protect the environment, or keep it safe.

Facing the Facts

Cows burp out a gas called methane that helps the **atmosphere** trap heat. The more cows there are, the more methane there is, which is another reason why cutting down forests to raise cows hurts the environment.

Smog is fog mixed with air pollution.

Climate Change

One of the biggest problems activists are trying to fix is **climate** change. Different places have different climates, but they're all changing because of things humans are doing.

Using **fossil fuels** to power cars and airplanes, heat houses, and run factories releases gases, including carbon dioxide and carbon monoxide, into the air. Like methane, these gases trap heat in the atmosphere. As Earth warms up, all kinds of climates change. For example, warmer weather over a long time means snow and ice melt in some parts of the world. However, global warming can also cause bad snowstorms in some places.

Facing the Facts 🔍

Global warming is the warming of Earth over time. Earth's average **temperature** has gone up by about 1.8 degrees Fahrenheit (1 degree Celsius) since 1880.

WARMER AIR
HOLDS MORE MOISTURE

1°F (0.5°C) increase =
4% more water vapor

moisture

heavy
snow

heavier
rain

- temperature +

Warmer weather causes worse snowstorms,
thunderstorms, and **hurricanes**. This is because
warmer air holds more water vapor—water as a gas.

Pollution

Gases from burning fossil fuels don't just make the planet warmer. They also pollute the air, making it hard for people and animals to breathe. In fact, the World Health **Organization** (WHO) says that 4.2 million people die because of outdoor air pollution every year. This makes it one of the most common causes of death in the world.

People also pollute the water by dumping garbage or deadly **chemicals** into it. This makes it dangerous, or unsafe, for people to drink the water in some places. It also kills the plants and animals that live in or near the water.

Facing the Facts

There's a lot of plastic in the ocean, and more than half of it floats. Ocean currents push it together into five large areas called patches. The largest is the Great Pacific Garbage Patch, which is twice the size of Texas!

ASIA

EUROPE

NORTH
AMERICA

GREAT PACIFIC
GARBAGE PATCH

AFRICA

SOUTH
AMERICA

AUSTRALIA

ANTARCTICA

Garbage from the Great
Pacific Garbage Patch often
washes up on beaches.

Environmental Groups

Some environmental activists work together in organizations to conserve, or protect, the environment. The largest one is the World Wildlife Fund (WWF). This organization mainly works to protect animals that are endangered, or close to dying out. Its members lobby, or talk to, governments to ask them to pass laws that protect animals.

Other environmental organizations include Greenpeace, Climate Foundation, Rainforest Action Network, and Friends of the Earth. These and dozens of other groups work to **convince** people and governments that changes need to be made in the way people in most parts of the world live.

Facing the Facts 🔍

Most people first heard about Rainforest Action Network in 1987. That year, the group convinced Burger King not to order its beef from Central America because the farmers there were cutting down too many trees for their cows.

Early environmental activist John Muir created an environmental organization called the Sierra Club in 1892.

Other Activists

Not all activists are part of organizations. One of the most famous environmental activists today is Greta Thunberg. Thunberg, who is Swedish, became famous when she was 15 because she **protested** outside a Swedish government building. The goal of her protest was to get Swedish leaders to pass laws to fight climate change.

Another famous young activist is Hans Cosmas Ngoteya from Tanzania. He cofounded an organization called Landscape and Conservation **Mentors**. This group helps communities make changes that protect the environment while also making money they can use to help the people who live there.

Facing the Facts 🔍

Jane Goodall has been an environmental activist since the 1970s. She worked with chimpanzees in Tanzania, and in 1977, she set up an organization to protect them and their habitat, or natural home.

Greta Thunberg has given speeches to protesters as well as the United Nations (UN).

Working Toward Change

Environmental activists are trying to change a lot of things. They're working to protect the air and water we need to live. They're also working to make sure humans don't harm animals and plants. They want governments to pass laws that help with these goals.

Activists also want to convince people to do the right thing no matter what the laws are. For example, people don't go to jail for littering, but it's still wrong! It can hurt plants and animals who eat or get caught in the garbage on the ground.

Facing the Facts

One thing activists want people to do is recycle or reuse things. Recycling puts less carbon dioxide into the atmosphere than making new items does.

When garbage ends up in the ocean, it kills a lot of animals that mistake it for food, such as sea turtles that eat jellyfish.

Small and Big

To protect the environment, activists say we need a mix of small and big actions. Everyone needs to pitch in and help out by recycling and reusing things, saving water, not littering, and other small actions. However, governments also need to pass laws that protect the environment and stop large companies from hurting it.

Switching from fossil fuels to solar, wind, or water power is one way companies can help. These are called "clean" power sources because they don't pollute the air with carbon gases. Companies can also fix machines when they break instead of throwing them out and getting new ones.

Facing the Facts

Since 1988, more than 70 percent of the carbon gases put into the atmosphere have come from just 100 of the world's companies.

Solar panels (shown here) take in sunlight and turn it into energy, or power.

How to Help

There are a lot of things you can do to help protect the environment. You can turn the water off while you brush your teeth, recycle when you can, and ride your bike or walk to places that are close by instead of taking a car or bus.

You can also join environmental activists in their fight to get governments and companies to be more environmentally friendly. Ask a trusted adult to take you to a protest, or write a letter to your elected officials letting them know you support laws that protect the environment.

Facing the Facts 🔍

The United States has 5 percent of the world's population but throws out 30 percent of the world's garbage.

WHAT CAN YOU DO?

Only buy things from people and companies that are working to be environmentally friendly.

Go to an environmental protest.

Walk or ride your bike when it's safe to do so.

Ask your parents or guardians about powering your home with clean energy.

Turn off lights when you leave a room.

Reuse and recycle whenever you can.

You don't have to be a famous environmental activist to make a difference. Every day, we can make choices to help protect the environment.

GLOSSARY

atmosphere: The mixture of gases that surround a planet.

chemical: Any substance that is formed when two or more other substances act upon one another or one that is used to produce a change in another substance.

climate: The weather in a place over a long period of time.

convince: To argue to make a person agree with or believe something.

disrupt: To interrupt the normal course of.

fossil fuel: A fuel (such as coal, oil, or natural gas) formed in the earth from dead plants or animals.

hurricane: A tropical storm with very high winds, rain, thunder, and lightning.

mentor: A trusted guide.

nutrient: A substance that is needed for healthy growth, development, and functioning.

organization: A group of people united for a common purpose.

protest: To take part in an event in which people gather to show disapproval of something, or the event itself.

temperature: How hot or cold something is.

transportation: Ways of moving people or goods from one place to another.

FOR MORE INFORMATION

WEBSITES

NASA Climate Kids

climatekids.nasa.gov

Read more about the science behind climate change.

Young Voices for the Planet

www.youngvoicesfortheplanet.com/for-kids/

Learn about ways you can take action to save the planet.

BOOKS

Debbink, Andrea, and Asia Orlando. *The Wild World Handbook: How Adventurers, Artists, Scientists—and You—Can Protect Earth's Habitats.* Philadelphia, PA: Quirk Books, 2021.

Sarah, Rachel. *Girl Warriors: How 25 Young Activists Are Saving the Earth.* Chicago, IL: Chicago Review Press, 2021.

Stevens, Georgina, and Katie Rewse. *Climate Action: The Future Is in Our Hands.* Wilton, CT: 360 Degrees, 2021.

INDEX